MILLION DOLLAR MISTAKES

How Entrepreneurs Survived and Built Empires

MJ Gray

Million Dollar Mistakes:

How Entrepreneurs Survived and Built Empires

INTRODUCTION

Million Dollar Mistakes: How Entrepreneurs Survived and Built Empires

Tired of feeling trapped in a dead-end job? Dreaming of financial freedom and living life on your own terms? The truth is, millions are doing it right now, leveraging simple skills you already possess.

This book isn't about some get-rich quick scheme or overnight success. It's about unlocking the hidden potential within your everyday talents and transforming them into million-dollar opportunities. Packed with real-world stories, actionable strategies, and expert insights, this guide will show you how to:

Identify your million-dollar skill: Discover the hidden value in your hobbies, passions, and everyday strengths.

Turn your skill into a hustle: Learn how to package, market, and monetize your skill through various platforms and strategies.

Build a thriving community: Leverage the power of networks and collaborations to accelerate your growth and reach.

Design your dream lifestyle: Develop the financial mindset and habits needed to achieve lasting financial freedom.

Stop dreaming and start acting. Unleash your million-dollar potential, starting today!

PART1: THE MAKING OF AN ENTREPRENEUR

CHAPTER 1: FROM EMPLOYEE TO ENTREPRENEUR: THE LEAP OF FAITH

The office cubicle felt like a cage, the fluorescent lights buzzing a monotonous lullaby. Every day was a predictable march down the same well-worn path, each step towards a comfortable retirement that somehow felt distant and uninspiring. This was Sarah's reality, a successful marketing executive by all standards, yet yearning for something more. "Is this all there is?" the question echoed in her mind, fueled by the faint embers of an untamed dream – a bustling online clothing boutique catering to eco-conscious fashionistas.

Taking the leap from employee to entrepreneur is often described as a "leap of faith," a phrase loaded with both hope and trepidation. It's the moment you stand at the precipice, the chasm of the unknown yawning before you, the familiar ground of a steady paycheck and benefits receding into the distance. This chapter explores the motivations that propel individuals like Sarah to take this daunting plunge, the stark realities they face, and the essential qualities required to navigate this transformative journey.

Motivations: Whispers of Dreams and Yearnings

The reasons for leaving the comfort of employment are as diverse as the individuals themselves. For some, it's the thirst for freedom and control , a yearning to escape the rigid structures of corporate life and chart their own destiny. Sarah, like many others, dreamt of being her own boss, setting her own schedule, and building something that embodied her values.

"I couldn't shake the feeling that someone else was holding the remote to my life," admits David, a former software engineer who traded in his cubicle for the freedom of freelance web development. "Now, I get to choose the projects I work on, the hours I keep, and the impact I make."

Beyond freedom, many are driven by a burning desire to pursue a passion long relegated to the back burner. Perhaps it's a hidden talent waiting to blossom, a creative itch demanding to be scratched, or a cause bigger than oneself yearning for championing. Maya, a former teacher, left the security of her profession to launch a non-profit organization promoting literacy in underprivileged communities. "The spark was always there," she shares, "but the stability of a paycheck held me back. Taking the leap allowed me to finally ignite that spark and watch it grow into something truly meaningful."

Financial independence, while not a guaranteed outcome, remains a powerful motivator for many. The possibility of breaking free from the paycheck-to-paycheck cycle and building wealth through one's own efforts holds immense allure. But beware, the entrepreneurial path is rarely paved with overnight riches. "It's not about getting rich quick," cautions Tom, a seasoned entrepreneur who built a successful consulting firm, "it's about building something sustainable, something that allows you to control your financial future and create the lifestyle you desire."

Ultimately, the most potent motivator may not be a single factor, but rather a confluence of desires and frustrations . The corporate hamster wheel starts to feel less exhilarating and more monotonous, the dissatisfaction with the status quo grows, and the whispers of unfulfilled dreams become too loud to ignore. The "leap of faith" becomes not just a jump, but a calculated response to a deeper calling.

Facing the Realities: Risks and Rewards on the Tightrope

The decision to step off the ledge isn't made lightly. Entrepreneurship is a tightrope walk, the wind of uncertainty whistling past your ears as you strive for balance between risks and rewards .

On one side, the chasm of financial instability looms large. Sarah, juggling her online store with part-time freelance work, acknowledges the initial financial strain. "There were months when I questioned every decision," she admits, "but the passion kept me going, and slowly, the financial rewards started trickling in." Long hours and relentless hard work become your companions, testing your dedication and resilience. David, the ex-engineer, recalls countless nights fueled by coffee and code, "There were times when I missed the structure of a 9-to-5, but the satisfaction of seeing my own business grow kept me pushing."

Uncertainty is another constant companion. Unlike the predictable trajectory of a corporate career, the entrepreneurial journey is a winding path , fraught with unexpected turns and potential pitfalls. Market shifts, fierce competition, and unforeseen challenges can threaten even the most meticulously planned ventures. But within this uncertainty lies the seeds of opportunity . Adaptability becomes your superpower, allowing you to pivot strategies, embrace change, and seize emerging possibilities.

The weight of these risks can be daunting, but let's not forget the rewards on the other side. The freedom to pursue your passions, the flexibility to design your own work-life balance, and the satisfaction of building something from the ground up are powerful motivators. Tom, reflecting on his journey, smiles ...and smiles, "The greatest reward? Knowing that every success, every milestone, is a direct result of your own effort, your own vision. It's a feeling of accomplishment no corporate promotion can match."

Beyond Passion and Dreams: The Essential Traits for Success

While the allure of freedom and potential rewards beckons, not everyone is cut out for the entrepreneurial rollercoaster . Before taking the leap, it's crucial to honestly assess your personal qualities and determine if you possess the essential traits for success.

Resilience: The path is rarely smooth, paved with setbacks, failures, and moments of self-doubt. Sarah recalls early product launches that flopped, technical glitches that caused sleepless nights, and periods of self-reflection where she questioned her decision. "But," she emphasizes, "the ability to bounce back, learn from mistakes, and keep moving forward is what separates those who succeed from those who give up."

Adaptability: The business landscape is dynamic, and those who cling to rigidity will be left behind. David thrives on the constant evolution of his industry, embracing new technologies and adapting his services to cater to changing client needs. "Entrepreneurship is like surfing," he says, "you have to learn to read the waves and adjust your approach accordingly."

Resourcefulness: Bootstrapping is often the name of the game, demanding creativity and resourcefulness. Tom remembers bartering services, utilizing free online tools, and leveraging social media to reach his target audience. "You learn to think outside the box, use limited resources to your advantage, and get things done with a bit of ingenuity."

Self-motivation: The corporate world provides external motivators – deadlines, performance reviews, and appraisals. In the entrepreneurial realm, the buck stops with you. Maintaining intrinsic motivation, staying focused on your vision, and pushing forward even when the going gets tough is crucial. Maya draws inspiration from the impact her organization creates, "Seeing the faces of children learning to read fuels my fire every day, even when fundraising gets challenging."

Risk Tolerance: Not everyone enjoys the thrill of a tightrope walk. Embracing calculated risks is essential, understanding that not every venture will succeed. The key lies in learning from failures, mitigating risks where possible, and having a healthy dose of optimism to propel you forward.

Remember: This is just a starting point. Tailor these traits and examples to resonate with your target audience and their specific aspirations.

The Road Ahead: Embracing the Journey

Taking the leap from employee to entrepreneur is a monumental decision, a journey filled with both exhilarating highs and gut-wrenching lows. It's about more than just chasing dreams or seeking financial freedom; it's about embracing a different way of being , a path of self-discovery, growth, and constant learning.

As you ponder your own leap of faith, remember this: preparation is key . Research your industry, develop a sound business plan, and surround yourself with supportive mentors and resources. Be realistic about the challenges you'll face, but never lose sight of the passion that ignited the flames of your entrepreneurial spirit.

This book will serve as your guide, offering not just practical advice and actionable steps, but also the stories and experiences of those who have walked this path before you. Remember, the leap of faith isn't a blind jump; it's a calculated step, fueled by passion, fueled by preparation, and guided by the unwavering belief in the power of your dreams.

Are you ready to take the leap? if yes, then let's go to

CHAPTER 2:

Dancing with Dragons: Passion, Profit, and the Entrepreneurial Tango

Ah, the siren song of entrepreneurship! Visions of freedom, impact, and self-actualization dance in your head, fueled by a passion that burns brighter than a dragon's breath. But hold on, intrepid adventurer, before you charge headfirst into this fantastical realm, let's talk about a crucial dance – the tango between passion and profit.

The Allure of the Fiery Passion:

Remember Sarah, the eco-conscious fashionista from Chapter 1? Her heart brimmed with a desire to empower consumers and champion sustainability. That's the magic of passion – it ignites your soul, propels you through late nights, and fuels resilience in the face of setbacks. It's like that feeling you get when a song perfectly captures your emotions, sending shivers down your spine and urging you to move.

But here's the thing: passion alone won't pay the bills. Imagine Sarah pouring her heart and soul into her online store, neglecting market research and pricing strategies. The initial excitement might fade as bills pile up, and the dream starts to resemble a financial nightmare. This, my friends, is the cautionary tale of mistaking passion for a business plan.

The Pragmatic Power of Profit:

Let's not demonize profit. It's not a dirty word; it's the lifeblood of your business. Think of it as the sturdy boots that allow you to explore the fantastical landscapes of your dreams without getting bogged down in financial quicksand. Profit fuels growth, empowers you to invest in better resources, and ultimately transforms your passion project into a sustainable reality.

Finding the Sweet Spot: The Entrepreneurial Tango:

So, how do we navigate this delicate dance? How do we harness the fiery passion without getting scorched by the harsh realities of profit? Here's where the real tango begins, a graceful interplay between the two:

1. Validate Your Dragon:

Not all dragons are Smaug hoarding treasure. Some, like Mushu from Mulan, bring good luck and guidance. Before embarking on your entrepreneurial quest, validate your passion with market research . Is there a real need for your product or service? Will people pay for it? Remember, Sarah didn't just follow her passion blindly; she researched eco-conscious fashion trends and identified a niche market craving stylish and sustainable options.

2. Craft Your Business Armor:

Passion is your sword, but a solid business plan is your shield. This plan outlines your value proposition, pricing strategy, customer acquisition strategy, and operational costs. How will you turn your fire into something people are willing to pay for? Think of Tom, the consultant from Chapter 1. He didn't just offer freelance services; he developed a unique package catering to specific client needs, ensuring both value and profitability.

3. Embrace the Agile Dragon:

Markets are like mythical beasts – constantly changing and evolving. Clinging to a rigid plan is like wearing armor two sizes too small. Be adaptable ! Embrace innovation, experiment with different marketing strategies, and learn from your customers. David, the web developer, constantly updates his skills, adapts to new technologies, and experiments with different marketing strategies to stay ahead of the curve.

4. Build Your Support Squad:

No knight slays dragons alone. Surround yourself with a community of mentors, advisors, and fellow entrepreneurs . They'll be your cheerleaders, wisdom-sharers, and occasional fire extinguishers when your passion gets a little too intense. Maya, from Chapter 1, found a network of other non-profit leaders who offered invaluable advice and collaboration opportunities, helping her organization thrive despite resource constraints.

Remember: This is an ongoing dance, not a one-time performance. Be prepared to reassess and adjust your approach as your business evolves and market conditions change. Think of it as refining your footwork, learning from each misstep, and ultimately creating a graceful and successful entrepreneurial tango.

Real-Life Dragonslayers: Balancing Passion and Profit:

Let's peek into the lairs of successful entrepreneurs who mastered this dance:

Blake Mycoskie, TOMS: Driven by a passion for helping others, Mycoskie started TOMS with a simple idea: for every pair of shoes purchased, a pair would be donated. This blended his passion for social impact with a profitable business model, creating a brand beloved by consumers and praised for its positive impact.

Jessica Alba, The Honest Company: Combining her desire for safe and healthy products for her family with a growing market for eco-friendly alternatives, Alba launched The Honest Company. Focusing on transparency and quality ingredients, she built a profitable business driven by her personal passion and aligned with consumer values.

Chipotle Mexican Grill, Steve Ells: Ells' vision of serving fresh, high-quality food at affordable prices fueled Chipotle's rise. Despite facing criticism for higher costs, his commitment to ethical sourcing and sustainable practices resonated with customers, proving that profit and purpose can coexist.

Patagonia, Yvon Chouinard: A renowned climber and environmentalist, Chouinard established Patagonia based on his passion for outdoor activities and protecting the environment. The company prioritizes environmental responsibility while remaining profitable, demonstrating that sustainability can be a driver of success.

Beyond the Stage: A Glimpse into the Future:

This chapter has explored the passionate tango with profit, but remember, this is just the first act in your entrepreneurial play. As you turn the page, prepare to encounter:

The treacherous terrain of Imposter Syndrome: We'll slay

the self-doubt dragon and develop the unshakeable confidence needed to thrive.

The ever-shifting sands of marketing: Learn to navigate the ever-evolving marketing landscape and attract your ideal customers like a siren song.

The mythical beast of funding: We'll explore diverse funding options and help you secure the resources to fuel your entrepreneurial fire.

The dance with failure: Learn to embrace setbacks as stepping stones, not roadblocks, and rise like a phoenix from the ashes.

So, dear adventurer, strap on your boots, grab your metaphorical sword (a well-crafted business plan, of course!), and prepare to embark on a journey filled with passion, purpose, and, most importantly, the knowledge to transform your dreams into a thriving reality. Remember, the entrepreneurial tango is a dance for the bold, the resilient, and those who dare to chase their dragons, not run from them.

Call to Action:

Before you step onto the dance floor, take a moment to reflect:

What is the burning passion that fuels your entrepreneurial dream?

Have you validated your idea with thorough market research?

Do you have a solid business plan that outlines your value proposition and financial strategy?

Are you prepared to adapt, learn, and grow as your business evolves?

Answering these questions will equip you with the initial steps needed to navigate the passionate tango with profit. Remember, the journey ahead will be filled with challenges, but with the right mindset and the knowledge gleaned from this chapter, you can turn your entrepreneurial dream into a roaring success.

CHAPTER 3:

Ditch the Hustle Myth: Work Smarter, Not Harder

Remember the gloriously romanticized image of the sleep-deprived entrepreneur, fueled by ramen and ambition, constantly grinding away? Forget it. While short bursts of intense effort can be productive, the constant glorification of the "hustle culture" paints an unrealistic and potentially harmful picture. This chapter aims to empower you to build a successful business without sacrificing your well-being or sanity. Let's dismantle the hustle myth and pave the way for a sustainable, fulfilling entrepreneurial journey.

Burnout: The Unseen Cost of the Hustle:

Dedication and effort are crucial for entrepreneurial success, but mistaking relentless busyness for productivity leads to a dangerous path. Burnout , characterized by emotional exhaustion, cynicism, and reduced effectiveness, is a real threat lurking behind the hustle culture facade. Think foggy brains, emotional detachment, and a dwindling spark for what once ignited your passion. Remember Sarah from Chapter 1? Initially, she embraced the "always-on" mentality, only to realize it was slowly chipping away at her creativity and joy. It wasn't until she prioritized rest and personal time that her passion reignited.

Work-Life Balance: Not Just for Yogis:

Achieving work-life balance isn't some unattainable ideal for privileged few; it's a strategic necessity for long-term entrepreneurial success. Neglecting personal life, family, and hobbies isn't just about missing out on fun; it creates a breeding ground for stress, isolation, and ultimately, decreased productivity and performance . Think of it like this: a well-rested, emotionally balanced you is a far more creative, efficient, and innovative you. Imagine David, the web developer, constantly sacrificing sleep and social time to squeeze in extra coding hours. While his dedication is admirable, it's likely affecting his focus, creativity, and ability to connect with clients. A strategic approach prioritizing sleep and social interaction could lead to more insightful solutions and deeper client relationships.

So, How Do We Ditch the Hustle?

Let's move beyond the glorified grind and create sustainable entrepreneurial lives. Here's your action plan:

1. Define Your "Winning": What does success look like YOU ? Is it a corner office and a six-figure salary, or more time with loved ones and pursuing your passions? Knowing your values helps you prioritize tasks and avoid getting sucked into the "more is more" trap . Remember Tom, the consultant, from Chapter 1? Recognizing his value for family time, he strategically delegated tasks and set clear boundaries, allowing him to achieve financial goals while enjoying cherished moments with his family.

2. Boundaries? You Betcha: Learn to say no gracefully. Set clear boundaries between work and personal time. Schedule sacred blocks for relaxation, hobbies, and family. Treat them like VIP appointments you can't miss. Maya, the non-profit leader, faced constant demands, but by setting clear boundaries

and communicating them effectively, she protected her personal time and prevented burnout, ensuring she could show up with renewed energy for her community.

3. Delegate Like a Boss: You don't have to be a one-person show. Embrace the power of delegation and outsourcing. Identify tasks that don't require your unique skills and delegate them to trusted individuals or freelancers. Sarah, the eco-fashion entrepreneur, initially handled everything from website design to social media. Delegating non-essential tasks freed up her time and allowed her to focus on her strengths, like product development and customer engagement.

4. Tech Is Your Friend: Leverage technology to your advantage. Use automation tools to streamline repetitive tasks like scheduling, social media management, and data entry. Think of it like giving yourself superpowers; David, the web developer, automated website maintenance tasks, freeing up his time for more strategic and creative projects.

5. Self-Care Ain't Selfish: Prioritizing your physical and mental well-being isn't a luxury; it's an investment in your success and happiness. Engage in regular exercise, eat nutritious foods, and make mindfulness practices a part of your routine. Remember, you're not a machine; you need to refuel and recharge to function at your best. Taking care of yourself is essential for sustainable success and long-term motivation.

Remember: Building sustainable habits takes time and effort. Experiment, find what works for you, and don't be afraid to adjust as needed. Your journey is unique, so personalize your approach and celebrate the small wins along the way.

Real Talk: Success Without the Hustle:

Numerous successful entrepreneurs have proven that you can ditch the hustle myth and prioritize balance. Here are some inspiring examples:

Tim Ferriss: This author and entrepreneur advocates for efficiency and automation to achieve financial freedom while living a fulfilling life (goodbye, 4-Hour Workweek!).

Sheryl Sandberg: The COO of Facebook champions the importance of work-life balance for women in leadership roles, proving success doesn't have to come at the expense of personal well-being.

Richard Branson: This iconic entrepreneur famously prioritizes adventure, travel, and family time alongside running his Virgin Group empire, demonstrating that a balanced life can fuel creativity and success.

Jessica Alba: The actress and founder of The Honest Company advocates for sustainable business practices and family time , proving financial success can co-exist with ethical values and a healthy personal life.

Satya Nadella: The CEO of Microsoft transformed the company culture to prioritize employee well-being and work-life balance , leading to increased productivity and innovation.

Remember, these are just a few examples. Countless other entrepreneurs navigate the business world successfully while prioritizing personal well-being and avoiding the unsustainable hustle culture. Their stories serve as a powerful reminder that work doesn't have to define you; it should empower and fulfill you .

Shifting Gears: From Hype to Habits

Now, let's move beyond mere inspiration and equip you with actionable strategies to ditch the hustle myth and cultivate sustainable success:

1. Embrace the Micro-Audit: Conduct a regular personal and professional audit . Analyze your energy levels, productivity, and overall well-being. Identify areas where you're sacrificing self-care for busyness. This self-awareness is crucial for crafting a personalized plan.

2. Design Your Ideal Week: Imagine your ideal work-life balance . How much time do you allocate to work, personal pursuits, and rest? Schedule these blocks in your calendar like important appointments, treating them with equal respect.

3. Tame the Tech Tiger: Identify and implement time-management tools like calendar apps, project management software, and website blockers. Remember, technology should empower you, not enslave you.

4. Embrace the Power of "No": Saying no allows you to focus on high-impact activities and protects your valuable time. Practice declining requests gracefully yet firmly, prioritizing tasks aligned with your goals and well-being.

5. Celebrate Small Wins: Recognize and celebrate your progress, no matter how small. This reinforces positive habits and fuels your motivation to stick with your sustainable approach.

Remember: Ditching the hustle is a journey, not a destination. There will be setbacks and adjustments along the way. Be kind to yourself, celebrate your progress, and keep evolving your approach as your business and needs change.

Beyond the Chapter: A Glimpse into the Future:

This chapter provided tools to combat the hustle myth and prioritize well-being. As you turn the page, prepare to delve into additional strategies for building a thriving business:

Building a Powerful Network: Learn how to forge valuable connections and leverage the support of your entrepreneurial community.

Marketing Magic: Discover effective marketing strategies to reach your target audience and attract ideal customers.

The Art of Funding: Explore diverse funding options to fuel your business growth without sacrificing your values.

Weathering the Storm: Learn to navigate challenges, overcome setbacks, and emerge stronger as an entrepreneur.

Remember, the journey to entrepreneurial success is paved with both triumphs and hurdles. Embrace the lessons, leverage the tools provided, and most importantly, prioritize your well-being to build a business that nourishes your soul and fuels your passion.

PART 2: LESSONS FROM THE TRENCHES

CHAPTER 4:

Million Dollar Mistakes: Learning from Failure

The entrepreneurial journey is often romanticized, painted with a rosy brush of overnight successes and meteoric rises. But the reality, as any seasoned adventurer knows, is a treacherous terrain littered with missteps, setbacks, and yes, even million-dollar mistakes.

However, fear not, intrepid explorer! For within these perceived failures lie untold riches . The scars and stumbles of those who dared to dream big and chase audacious goals offer invaluable lessons, waiting to be unearthed and transformed into stepping stones for future triumphs. In this chapter, we'll delve into the trenches of entrepreneurial battles, unearthing real-life tales of individuals who stumbled, fell, and ultimately emerged stronger, wiser, and wealthier – not just in finances, but in the invaluable knowledge they acquired.

From Stumbles to Stepping Stones: Real-Life Tales of Failure and Growth

Remember the epic blunder of Blockbuster rejecting Netflix's acquisition offer in 2000? A move initially celebrated as shrewd, it ultimately forced Netflix to innovate and embrace streaming, solidifying its position as the video-on-demand giant we know today. This wasn't a failure; it was a powerful pivot , a course correction fueled by adversity.

Think of Sara Blakely, the visionary behind Spanx. Before revolutionizing the shapewear industry, she faced countless rejections from manufacturers who deemed her idea "ridiculous." Yet, her unwavering belief in her product and relentless persistence led to the creation of a billion-dollar empire. Each "no" became a stepping stone, each rejection a lesson in resilience and determination.

Even the audacious Richard Branson, whose Virgin Group spans industries from airlines to music, hasn't been immune to missteps. From a near-bankruptcy in the 90s to the tragic loss of Virgin Galactic's SpaceShipTwo in 2014, Branson has faced his share of setbacks. However, his resilience, adaptability, and unwavering commitment to his vision have kept Virgin Group soaring high. These are not failures; they are chapters in the ongoing saga of an entrepreneur who dares to push boundaries and learn from every experience.

Unearthing the Gems: Common Threads in Entrepreneurial Missteps

While the specifics of each entrepreneur's journey differ, several common threads often weave through their tales of million-dollar mistakes:

Ignoring Market Research: Like Sarah Blakely initially, overlooking valuable market insights can lead to products or services that miss the mark, resulting in wasted resources and missed opportunities. Remember, flying blind is a recipe for disaster , not innovation.

Underestimating the Power of Adaptability: In a world

that changes faster than a chameleon's complexion, clinging to outdated strategies or being inflexible in the face of change can spell disaster. Remember Blockbuster's resistance to streaming? Agility is not a luxury; it's a survival skill in the entrepreneurial arena.

Neglecting Financial Planning: Poor financial management, inadequate funding, or unrealistic projections can quickly sink even the most promising ventures. Remember the importance of a solid business plan , not just a dream scribbled on a napkin. Treat your finances with the same respect you treat your product or service.

Failing to Build a Strong Team: Surrounding yourself with the right talent is crucial for success. Ignoring team dynamics, overlooking expertise, or fostering a toxic work environment can hinder progress. Remember, you're not a one-person show . Build a team that complements your skills and shares your vision.

Learning from the Masters: Key Takeaways for Aspiring Entrepreneurs

By studying the missteps of others, we can gain valuable wisdom to guide our own journeys:

Embrace Market Research: Conduct thorough research to understand your target audience, their needs, and existing solutions. Validate your idea before investing significant resources. Don't be afraid to ask questions, gather data, and iterate based on feedback .

Be Adaptable and Agile: Stay informed about industry trends, be prepared to pivot when necessary, and experiment with innovative approaches. Embrace change as an opportunity, not an obstacle . Remember, the only constant is change itself.

Prioritize Financial Planning: Develop a realistic and comprehensive financial plan, secure adequate funding, and track your progress meticulously. Don't be afraid to seek guidance from financial experts and remember, responsible spending is just as important as ambitious dreams.

Build a Dream Team: Surround yourself with talented, passionate individuals who complement your skills and share your vision. Foster a collaborative and supportive work environment where everyone feels valued and heard. Remember, your team is your greatest asset.

Learn from Failure: View setbacks as opportunities for growth. Analyze what went wrong, learn from the experience, and don't be afraid to try again.

Beyond the Lessons: Embracing the "Fail Forward" Mindset

Embracing a "fail forward" mindset is crucial for navigating the unpredictable terrain of entrepreneurship. This means viewing failures as learning experiences, not dead ends. It's about acknowledging missteps, extracting valuable lessons, and using them to fuel your next attempt.

Here are some keys to cultivating this resilient mindset:

Celebrate Small Wins: Don't wait for major successes to celebrate. Recognize and acknowledge progress, no matter how small. This reinforces a positive mindset and fuels your motivation to persevere.

Reframe Your Perspective: Instead of viewing setbacks as failures, see them as detours or learning opportunities. Ask yourself: "What can I learn from this experience? How can I use this knowledge to improve next time?"

Focus on Progress, Not Perfection: Striving for perfection can lead to paralysis and missed opportunities. Embrace the iterative nature of entrepreneurship and focus on making progress, not achieving instant perfection.

Seek Support and Feedback: Surround yourself with a network of mentors, advisors, and fellow entrepreneurs who can offer support, guidance, and valuable feedback. Don't be afraid to share your challenges and learn from others' experiences.

Maintain a Sense of Humor: Let's face it, things don't always go according to plan. Maintaining a sense of humor can help you de-stress, stay positive, and bounce back from setbacks with resilience.

Remember: The entrepreneurial journey is a marathon, not a sprint. There will be moments of doubt, setbacks, and even million-dollar mistakes. But by embracing a "fail forward" mindset, learning from the experiences of others, and implementing the strategies outlined above, you can transform these stumbling blocks into stepping stones that pave the way for a thriving and fulfilling entrepreneurial journey.

Case Studies: From Fumbles to Fortunes

To further illustrate the power of learning from failure, let's delve deeper into specific cases where individuals transformed mistakes into million-dollar successes:

Airbnb: Brian Chesky and Joe Gebbia's initial idea of renting out their apartment to make ends meet faced initial skepticism. However, their adaptability and willingness to pivot led them to expand their concept and target travelers, creating a hospitality empire valued at over $100 billion.

Dropbox: Drew Houston's flash drive mishap at MIT sparked the idea for Dropbox. However, initial prototypes were met with limited interest. By listening to user feedback and iterating on the product, he created a cloud storage solution that revolutionized file sharing and secured a multi-billion dollar valuation.

Slack: Stewart Butterfield's online game venture initially failed. However, he learned from this experience and used the platform's underlying technology to create Slack, a communication tool now used by millions of businesses worldwide.

Remember: These are just a few examples. Countless other entrepreneurs have turned setbacks into springboards for success. Their stories serve as a powerful reminder that mistakes are inevitable, but they don't have to define your journey. By learning from them, adapting, and persevering, you can transform them into stepping stones on your path to entrepreneurial success.

A Final Note: Your Entrepreneurial Odyssey Awaits

This chapter has delved into the sometimes messy, yet invaluable world of entrepreneurial failures. Remember, as you embark on your own journey, embrace the lessons learned, cultivate a "fail forward" mindset, and above all, never lose sight of your passion and determination. The path may be unpredictable, but with resilience, adaptability, and the wisdom gleaned from the trenches, you can transform million-dollar mistakes into stepping stones towards building a thriving and fulfilling entrepreneurial future.

CHAPTER 5:

Overcoming Obstacles: Turning Setbacks into Stepping Stones

The entrepreneurial path, despite its alluring promise of freedom and success, is paved with obstacles. From funding crunches and market shifts to team disagreements and burnout, challenges are inevitable. But fear not, intrepid adventurer! This chapter equips you with the mindset and tools to transform setbacks into stepping stones, navigate rough terrain, and emerge stronger, wiser, and more resilient.

The Inevitable Dance with Adversity:

Remember Maya, the passionate leader from Chapter 1? Despite her dedication, her non-profit faced funding cuts and volunteer burnout. This is the reality: obstacles are not roadblocks; they're part of the dance. Imagine Steve Jobs, facing multiple firings and setbacks before ultimately revolutionizing the tech industry. He, like countless others, learned to embrace adversity, adapt, and ultimately triumph.

Shifting Your Perspective: From Fear to Fuel:

Our initial reaction to challenges is often fear or discouragement. But what if we could reframe setbacks as opportunities for growth? Remember Sarah, the eco-fashion entrepreneur from Chapter 1? When faced with production delays, she saw it as a chance to improve her supply chain and build stronger relationships with vendors. This shift in perspective transformed a potential obstacle into a valuable learning experience.

Building Your Resilience Toolkit:

Now, let's equip you with practical strategies to navigate challenges with grace and grit:

1. Embrace Your Inner "Why": Reconnect with your passion and purpose. Why did you embark on this entrepreneurial journey? When challenges threaten to dim your fire, rekindling your "why" fuels your resilience and reminds you of the bigger picture.

2. Develop a Growth Mindset: Believe that your abilities can be developed through effort and experience. Embrace challenges as opportunities to learn and grow, not proof of your inadequacy. Think of David, the web developer, who initially struggled with a demanding client. He approached the situation as a learning opportunity, honing his communication skills and project management expertise.

3. Cultivate Grit and Determination: Setbacks are inevitable, but letting them define you is optional. Develop grit, the perseverance to push through challenges and keep moving forward, even when things get tough. Think of Tom, the consultant, who faced rejection after rejection before securing his first major client. His unwavering determination ultimately paved the way for his success.

4. Build a Support Network: Surround yourself with positive,

supportive individuals who believe in you and your vision. Mentors, fellow entrepreneurs, and even friends and family can offer invaluable guidance, encouragement, and a listening ear during tough times. Remember Maya, who leaned on her network of other nonprofit leaders to navigate funding challenges and develop innovative solutions.

5. Learn from Failure: Don't dwell on mistakes; analyze them, learn from them, and move forward . Ask yourself: "What went wrong? What could I have done differently?" This growth-oriented approach transforms failures into stepping stones for future success. Remember Richard Branson, whose Virgin Galactic faced a tragic setback. He channeled his grief into creating a foundation for space safety, demonstrating true resilience and a commitment to learning from adversity.

Navigating the Unexpected: Adaptability is Key:

The business landscape is a chameleon, constantly shifting and evolving. Clinging to rigid plans in the face of change is a recipe for disaster. Cultivate adaptability , the ability to adjust your strategies and approach based on new information and circumstances . Think of Chipotle, which faced criticism for its higher prices. Instead of ignoring feedback, they doubled down on their commitment to sustainable ingredients and ethical sourcing, resonating with customers who valued these principles.

Building Mental Fortitude: Resilience is Your Armor:

Burnout and negativity can chip away at even the most determined entrepreneur. To combat this, prioritize mental well-being :

Practice mindfulness and relaxation techniques: Meditation, yoga, or deep breathing can help manage stress and maintain focus.

Engage in activities you enjoy: Take breaks, pursue hobbies, and nurture your passions. Remember, neglecting your well-being diminishes your capacity to tackle challenges.

Celebrate small wins: Acknowledge your progress, no matter how small. Recognizing your achievements fosters a sense of accomplishment and boosts motivation.

Seek professional help if needed: Don't hesitate to seek professional support if you're struggling with overwhelming stress or negativity.

Real-Life Resilience: Inspiration from the Trenches:

Let's draw inspiration from entrepreneurs who weathered storms and emerged stronger:

Oprah Winfrey: Overcoming poverty, racism, and sexual abuse, Oprah built a media empire through sheer determination and resilience.

JK Rowling: Facing rejection from countless publishers, her Harry Potter series went on to become a global phenomenon, a testament to perseverance.

Elon Musk: From the near-bankruptcy of Tesla to SpaceX's early launch failures, Musk has faced and overcome numerous challenges, demonstrating unwavering grit and a willingness to learn from setbacks.

Amanda Gorman: Overcoming a speech impediment, Amanda blossomed into a powerful poet and activist, inspiring millions with her courage and resilience.

These are just a few examples. Countless entrepreneurs have walked through fire and emerged stronger, wiser, and more determined. Their stories serve as a powerful reminder that obstacles are not roadblocks; they are opportunities to forge your own path and build resilience you never knew you possessed.

Beyond the Tools: Embracing the Hero's Journey:

Think of your entrepreneurial journey as a hero's myth, filled with trials, triumphs, and moments of self-discovery. Challenges are not there to break you, but to shape you into the hero of your own story . Remember, the greatest heroes are not those who avoid challenges, but those who overcome them with courage, resilience, and a spirit of unwavering determination.

Remember: The path to entrepreneurial success is not linear. There will be moments of doubt, setbacks, and even tears. But by embracing the strategies outlined in this chapter, cultivating a growth mindset, and surrounding yourself with a supportive network, you can transform obstacles into stepping stones and emerge from the trenches stronger, wiser, and more resilient than ever before..

CHAPTER 6:

The Power of Persistence: When "No" Means "Next"

Imagine yourself standing at the foot of a mountain, your gaze fixed on the summit. The path ahead is steep, littered with boulders and treacherous stretches. Doubt whispers in your ear, "Turn back, it's too hard." But deep within, a fire burns - the unwavering belief in your dream, the vision that compels you to climb. This, dear reader, is the essence of persistence : the unwavering commitment to your vision, even when the world screams "no".

The Relentless Spirit of Entrepreneurs:

The entrepreneurial journey is rarely a fairytale of overnight success. It's a marathon, not a sprint, paved with countless rejections, setbacks, and moments of self-doubt. But what separates the victors from the vanquished is not the absence of challenges, but their relentless spirit , their unwavering persistence in the face of adversity .

Think of Walt Disney, facing countless rejections before securing funding for his first animation studio. His unwavering belief in his dream ultimately led to the creation of a magical empire that continues to inspire generations. Or consider Arianna Huffington, whose revolutionary idea for The Huffington Post was initially met with skepticism and laughter. Yet, she persisted, proving that even the most unconventional ideas can change the world.

Why "No" Means "Next":

Rejections and setbacks are inevitable, but they are not death sentences. They are simply   detours, not dead ends . When you hear "no", remember it doesn't mean your idea is bad, it just means it's not the right fit for that particular person or opportunity. View each "no" as a stepping stone, an opportunity to   refine your approach, learn, and grow .

Remember,   every successful entrepreneur has a collection of "no"s . J.K. Rowling's Harry Potter manuscript was rejected by 12 publishers before finding its home. Colonel Sanders received over 1,000 rejections for his Kentucky Fried Chicken recipe before landing his first franchise deal. These stories are not cautionary tales, but testaments to the power of persistence .

Fueling Your Inner Fire: Tips for Staying the Course:

Now, let's equip you with the tools to cultivate unwavering persistence in your entrepreneurial journey:

1. Define Your "Why":   What ignites your passion? Why are you embarking on this journey? Reconnect with your   core purpose during moments of doubt. Remember, a strong "why" fuels your resilience and keeps you moving forward even when the path gets tough.

2. Cultivate a Growth Mindset: Believe that your abilities and knowledge can be developed through effort and experience. View challenges as opportunities to learn and grow , not proof of your inadequacy. Remember, every obstacle holds a valuable lesson waiting to be unearthed.

3. Celebrate Small Wins: Don't wait for major milestones to celebrate. Acknowledge your progress, no matter how small. Recognizing your achievements fosters a sense of accomplishment and boosts your motivation to keep going.

4. Surround Yourself with Supportive People: Build a network of positive, encouraging individuals who believe in you and your vision. Mentors, fellow entrepreneurs, and even friends and family can offer invaluable guidance, encouragement, and a listening ear during tough times.

5. Develop Grit and Determination: Setbacks are inevitable, but letting them define you is optional. Cultivate grit, the perseverance to push through challenges and keep moving forward, even when things get tough. Remember, success rarely comes easy; it demands unwavering determination and the will to never give up.

6. Reframe Failure: Don't dwell on mistakes; analyze them, learn from them, and move forward . Ask yourself: "What went wrong? What could I have done differently?" This growth-oriented approach transforms failures into stepping stones for future success.

7. Practice Self-Care: Prioritize your mental and physical well-being. Engage in activities you enjoy, take breaks, and don't neglect your health . Remember, a burnt-out entrepreneur is an ineffective entrepreneur. Taking care of yourself fuels your resilience and ensures you have the energy to keep pushing forward.

Remember: The path to success is rarely linear. There will

be moments of doubt, setbacks, and tears. But by embracing the strategies outlined in this chapter, cultivating a growth mindset, and never losing sight of your "why", you can transform "no" into "next", turning rejections into stepping stones, and ultimately unlocking the power of persistence to achieve your entrepreneurial dreams.

Real-Life Perseverance: Stories of Grit and Determination:

Let's draw inspiration from entrepreneurs who turned "no" into a springboard for success:

Oprah Winfrey: Overcoming poverty, racism, and sexual abuse, Oprah built a media empire through sheer determination and resilience, facing countless rejections along the way.

Michael Jordan: Cut from his high school basketball team, Jordan channeled his disappointment into relentless practice, ultimately becoming one of the greatest basketball players of all time.

Thomas Edison: After failing over 10,000 times to create a light bulb, Edison famously said, "I haven't failed - I've just found 10,000 ways that won't work." This unwavering persistence led to the invention that revolutionized the world.

These are just a few examples. Countless entrepreneurs have walked through fire and emerged stronger, wiser, and more determined. Their stories serve as a powerful reminder that obstacles are not roadblocks; they are opportunities to forge your own path and build resilience you never knew you possessed.

Beyond the Tools: Embracing the Marathon Mindset:

Remember, the entrepreneurial journey is a marathon, not a sprint. There will be moments when doubt creeps in, when the finish line seems impossibly far away. But don't be discouraged by the length of the race; focus on the power of each step forward . Celebrate small victories, learn from setbacks, and keep moving forward, one determined step at a time.

Remember: Every "no" brings you closer to a "yes". Every obstacle strengthens your resolve. Every challenge refines your approach. Embrace the journey, cultivate the fire of persistence within you , and never lose sight of the dream that ignited your entrepreneurial spirit.

A Final Note: Leave Your Mark on the World:

The world needs your unique voice, your innovative ideas, your unwavering spirit. Don't let rejections and setbacks silence your dreams. Embrace the power of persistence, channel your "no"s into fuel, and leave your mark on the world through your relentless pursuit of your entrepreneurial vision.

>"The difference between ordinary and extraordinary is that little extra." - Jimmy Johnson

PART 3: MASTERING THE GAME

CHAPTER 7:

Building a Brand You Believe In: Crafting a Compass for Connection

In the ever-evolving landscape of business, standing out requires more than just a good product or service. It demands a powerful brand identity , a beacon that attracts your ideal audience and resonates with their values. This chapter serves as your guide to crafting a brand you believe in, a brand that builds trust and ignites connection .

From Blur to Beacon: Why Branding Matters

Imagine walking into a crowded marketplace. Every stall seems the same, a blur of noise and products. Then, you spot a vibrant banner, a unique logo, and a message that speaks directly to your needs. That's the power of a strong brand: it cuts through the clutter, captures attention, and builds trust.

Remember Steve Jobs' unboxing the first iPhone, not just introducing a device, but unveiling a lifestyle, a brand that symbolized innovation and sleek design. Or consider Patagonia, whose commitment to environmental activism resonates deeply with its audience, solidifying their position beyond just outdoor apparel. Branding is not just aesthetics; it's a story, a promise, a connection waiting to be forged.

The Anatomy of a Powerful Brand:

Before embarking on your branding journey, let's deconstruct the essential elements:

Core Values: What are the fundamental principles that drive your business? What values do you want to represent and embody? Be authentic, be clear, and let these values be the bedrock of your brand identity.

Mission Statement: What problem do you solve? What impact do you want to create? Craft a concise statement that encapsulates your purpose and motivates action.

Target Audience: Who are you trying to reach? Understand their needs, aspirations, and challenges. Speak their language, resonate with their values, and build a brand that feels like it was made for them.

Unique Value Proposition (UVP): What sets you apart? What makes your brand unique and irreplaceable? Clearly articulate your UVP and communicate it effectively.

Brand Voice and Personality: How do you want your brand to sound and feel? Are you friendly and approachable, or bold and innovative? Develop a consistent voice and personality that reflects your values and resonates with your audience.

Visual Identity: This includes your logo, colors, fonts, and overall aesthetic. Create a visually appealing and consistent brand identity that reinforces your message and leaves a lasting impression.

Beyond the Basics: Crafting a Story Worth Telling

Every successful brand tells a story. It's not just about selling a product or service; it's about connecting with your audience on an emotional level . Share your story, your journey, your passion.

What inspired you to start this business? What challenges have you overcome? What impact do you hope to make?

Remember, authenticity is key. People connect with real stories, real struggles, and real triumphs. Let your brand story be a window into your soul, a bridge that connects you to your audience on a deeper level.

Building Trust: The Cornerstone of Brand Success

In today's world, trust is currency. Consumers are bombarded with messages and claims, making them increasingly skeptical. So, how do you build trust with your brand?

Focus on Transparency: Be honest and upfront about your products, services, and practices. Don't make false promises or engage in misleading marketing.

Deliver on Your Promises: Ensure your products and services live up to the expectations set by your brand. Exceed expectations whenever possible.

Be Responsive and Engaged: Listen to your customers, address their concerns, and actively engage with them online and offline. Show them you care and value their feedback.

Stand for Something Bigger: Align your brand with a cause or movement that resonates with your values and target audience. This fosters a sense of connection and shared purpose.

Remember: Building trust takes time and effort. Be consistent, be genuine, and always strive to earn your audience's loyalty through transparency, integrity, and a commitment to their needs.

Real-Life Branding Lessons: Inspiration from the Masters

Let's learn from successful brands that have mastered the art of connection:

TOMS: Their "One for One" model, donating a pair of shoes for every purchase, resonates with socially conscious consumers who value purpose-driven brands.

GoPro: Their adventurous brand voice and user-generated content showcase the active lifestyle they enable, inspiring people to push their boundaries.

Dove: Their "Real Beauty" campaign challenged unrealistic beauty standards and empowered women to embrace their individuality, building trust through authenticity.

These are just a few examples. Look around, study, and be inspired by brands that resonate with you. Analyze what they do well, and adapt their strategies to fit your unique story and values.

Your Turn to Shine: Crafting Your Brand Compass

Now it's your turn to embark on your branding journey. Armed with the knowledge and tools presented in this chapter, take these steps to craft a brand that reflects your essence and connects with your ideal audience:

1. Conduct a Self-Discovery Audit:

Start with introspection: Define your core values, mission, and vision. What drives you? What impact do you want to make?

Know your audience: Conduct market research, understand

their needs, aspirations, and challenges. Create detailed buyer personas.

Identify your strengths: What makes you unique? What sets you apart from your competitors?

Craft your story: Capture your journey, your passion, and the reason behind your business.

2. Develop Your Brand Architecture:

Refine your core values and mission statement: Ensure they are concise, clear, and emotionally resonant.

Craft your UVP: Clearly articulate what makes your brand unique and irreplaceable.

Develop your brand voice and personality: Define how you want your brand to sound and feel. Choose words and phrases that reflect your values and resonate with your audience.

Design your visual identity: Create a logo, color palette, fonts, and overall aesthetic that are visually appealing, consistent, and reflect your brand personality.

3. Bring Your Brand to Life:

Create a brand style guide: This document outlines your brand voice, visuals, and messaging guidelines to ensure consistency across all platforms.

Develop a launch strategy: How will you introduce your brand to the world? Consider website relaunch, social media campaigns, or influencer partnerships.

Live your brand: Every interaction, from your website to customer service, should embody your brand values and personality.

Continuously evaluate and adapt: Track your brand performance, gather feedback, and be willing to evolve your brand as needed to stay relevant and connected to your audience.

Remember: Building a powerful brand is an ongoing journey, not a one-time destination. Be patient, be consistent, and most importantly, be authentic. When you create a brand that truly reflects your values and resonates with your audience, you'll build trust, foster connection, and ultimately achieve your entrepreneurial dreams.

A Final Note: Let Your Brand Shine:

In the ever-crowded marketplace, your brand is your beacon, your guiding light. It's not just a logo or tagline; it's the essence of your business, the story you tell, the connection you forge with your audience. Embrace the power of branding, pour your passion into it, and let your brand shine brightly, illuminating the path to your entrepreneurial success.

>"Your brand is the story you tell about yourself. Make it a good one." - Jeff Bezos

CHAPTER 8:

Networking for Success: Cultivating Meaningful Connections

In the intricate ecosystem of business, success rarely blossoms in isolation. Building a strong network, cultivating meaningful connections, and forging strategic partnerships are crucial ingredients for entrepreneurial growth. This chapter equips you with the strategies and mindset to transform networking from a daunting chore into a catalyst for collaboration, innovation, and mutual success.

Beyond Handshakes and Business Cards: The Power of Authentic Connection

Forget the outdated image of forced small talk and empty promises. Effective networking is about cultivating authentic connections , building genuine relationships based on shared values, mutual respect, and a desire for collaborative growth. It's about seeing others as collaborators, not competitors .

Consider Richard Branson, renowned entrepreneur and advocate for building bridges, not walls. His vast network, built on genuine connection and collaboration, has fueled the success of his diverse ventures. Or think of Sheryl Sandberg, who emphasizes the importance of "leaning in" and supporting other women entrepreneurs, creating a powerful network that fosters collective success.

Remember, networking is not a transaction; it's a relationship. Invest time in getting to know people, understand their interests and expertise, and offer genuine value before seeking anything in return.

Building Your Network Blueprint: From Seed to Forest

Now, let's equip you with the tools to cultivate a thriving network:

1. Define Your Goals: What do you hope to achieve through networking? New clients, strategic partnerships, industry insights, or mentorship? Clarity on your goals guides your approach and helps you identify relevant connections.

2. Identify Your Target Audience: Who are the people you want to connect with? Industry professionals, potential clients, investors, or mentors? Research, attend industry events, and join relevant online communities.

3. Start Small and Be Authentic: Don't overwhelm yourself trying to meet everyone at once. Start by connecting with individuals you share common interests or values with. Be genuine, engage in authentic conversations, and focus on building relationships, not just collecting contacts.

4. Give Before You Take: Networking is a two-way street. Offer your expertise, share valuable resources, and actively support others before seeking assistance. Remember, generosity fosters trust and reciprocity.

5. Leverage the Power of Online Communities: Utilize social

media platforms like LinkedIn and industry-specific forums to connect with professionals, participate in discussions, and showcase your expertise.

6. Join Professional Organizations and Attend Events: Participating in industry gatherings, conferences, and workshops allows you to meet like-minded individuals, exchange ideas, and build meaningful connections.

7. Nurture Your Network: Building relationships takes time and effort. Stay connected with your network through regular communication, offering support, and celebrating each other's successes.

Remember: Networking is not a one-time event; it's an ongoing process. Commit to cultivating genuine connections, offering value, and nurturing your network over time. The seeds you sow today will blossom into a forest of opportunities tomorrow.

The Art of Strategic Partnerships: Collaboration for Mutual Growth

Beyond individual connections, forging strategic partnerships can propel your business to new heights. Here's how:

1. Identify Potential Partners: Look for businesses that complement your skills and share your values. Consider collaborative projects, co-marketing initiatives, or joint ventures.

2. Define Clear Goals and Expectations: Ensure both parties have a shared understanding of the collaboration's goals, expectations, and responsibilities. Clear communication is key to a successful

partnership.

3. **Leverage Each Other's Strengths:** Play to each other's strengths and expertise. Combine your resources and skills to create something greater than either of you could achieve alone.

4. **Foster Open Communication and Trust:** Maintain open communication throughout the partnership, address challenges constructively, and build trust through transparency and mutual respect.

5. **Celebrate Successes and Learn from Challenges:** Recognize and celebrate achievements together. View challenges as opportunities for growth and learning, strengthening the partnership through shared experiences.

Remember: Strategic partnerships can unlock new markets, accelerate growth, and bring fresh perspectives to your business. Choose your partners wisely, invest in building trust, and leverage the power of collaboration to achieve mutual success.

Real-Life Collaboration Gems: Inspiration from Powerhouse Partnerships

Let's draw inspiration from successful partnerships that have reshaped industries:

Starbucks and Spotify: This collaboration offers Starbucks customers exclusive access to curated playlists based on their coffee choices, enhancing the customer experience and boosting brand loyalty for both companies.

Netflix and Marvel: This partnership resulted in

critically acclaimed television series like Daredevil and Jessica Jones, expanding Netflix's content library and bringing Marvel characters to life for a new generation.

Tesla and Panasonic: This strategic alliance focused on battery production, accelerating Tesla's electric vehicle production and contributing to sustainable mobility solutions.

Observe, analyze, and adapt: Look beyond these famous examples and explore collaborations within your own industry. Learn from their successes and challenges to inform your own partnership strategies.

Building Your Network Toolkit: Resources and Apps to Empower You:

In addition to the strategies outlined above, consider leveraging helpful resources and apps to streamline your networking journey:

LinkedIn: This professional networking platform allows you to connect with industry professionals, join relevant groups, and showcase your expertise.

Eventbrite: Discover industry events, workshops, and conferences to expand your network and connect with like-minded individuals.

Meetup: Join local or online communities based on your interests and expertise to connect with individuals who share your passions.

Calendly: Easily schedule and manage meetings with your network connections, ensuring efficiency and organization.

Buffer: Schedule and share valuable content across social media platforms, establishing yourself as a thought leader within your industry.

Remember: These tools are valuable resources, but they are not replacements for authentic connections. Use them strategically to enhance your networking efforts, not automate them.

A Final Note: Networking is a Journey, Not a Destination:

Building a strong network takes time, effort, and genuine commitment. Don't be discouraged by setbacks or slow progress. Celebrate small wins, nurture your connections, and embrace the journey of building meaningful relationships that will fuel your entrepreneurial success.

Embrace the Power of Connection:

In the closing words of Maya Angelou, "I've learned that people will forget what you said, people will forget what you did, but people will never forget how you made them feel." Let your networking efforts be guided by this sentiment. Foster genuine connections, offer value, and make others feel heard and supported. By building a network based on authenticity, respect, and collaboration, you'll not only unlock opportunities for yourself but also contribute to a more connected and supportive business ecosystem for everyone.

>"The network is your net worth." - Misha Burnett

CHAPTER 9:

Scaling Your Impact: From Solopreneur to Scalable BusinesS

You've achieved initial success as a solopreneur, but your vision burns bright, yearning to reach more people, create a bigger impact, and leave a lasting legacy. This chapter serves as your guide to scaling your business, transforming your solo operation into a well-oiled machine capable of reaching new heights.

Beyond Your Limits: Why Scale?

Imagine a lone lighthouse, guiding ships through the darkness. It fulfills a crucial purpose, but its reach is limited. Now, imagine a network of lighthouses, illuminating vast stretches of coastline, saving countless lives. Scaling your business is like expanding that lighthouse network, amplifying your impact and benefiting a wider audience.

Consider Elon Musk, not content with just building electric cars, but aiming to revolutionize transportation and space exploration. Or think of Oprah Winfrey, starting as a local news anchor and evolving into a media mogul, empowering millions through her voice and platform. Scaling allows you to multiply your impact, touch more lives, and truly fulfill your entrepreneurial vision.

The Crucial Shift: From "Me" to "We"

Scaling isn't just about growth; it's about a transition in mindset. As a solopreneur, you wear many hats, controlling every aspect. But to scale effectively, you need to move from "me" to "we", delegating tasks, building systems, and empowering others to share the journey.

Remember, you can't be everywhere, do everything, and maintain peak performance. Embrace collaboration, trust your team, and focus on your unique strengths to lead your business to greater heights.

Unlocking Growth: A Toolkit for Scaling Success

Now, let's explore various growth strategies and tools to navigate your scaling journey:

1. Define Your Growth Strategy: What does "scaling" mean for you? Expanding your product/service offerings, reaching new markets, or increasing brand awareness? Define your goals and choose strategies aligned with your vision.

2. Identify Your Scalable Offer: Not all products/services scale efficiently. Analyze your offerings and identify the ones with high growth potential. Consider recurring revenue models, digital products, or scalable service packages.

3. Leverage Systems and Automation: Repetitive tasks hinder scalability. Automate processes, create SOPs (Standard Operating Procedures), and invest in systems that free up your time and ensure consistent quality.

4. Build a High-Performing Team: You can't scale alone. Recruit talented individuals who share your values and vision. Invest in training, mentorship, and create a culture of collaboration and growth.

5. Delegate Effectively: Delegation isn't just assigning tasks; it's building trust and empowering others. Clearly communicate expectations, provide support, and celebrate successes to foster ownership and accountability.

6. Leverage Technology: Utilize technology to streamline operations, automate tasks, and reach a wider audience. Explore marketing automation tools, CRM systems, and project management platforms.

7. Partner with Strategic Allies: Collaboration can accelerate growth. Explore partnerships with complementary businesses, influencers, or industry leaders to expand your reach and tap into new markets.

8. Seek Funding (if applicable): Depending on your growth strategy, consider venture capital, angel investors, or crowdfunding to fuel expansion. Carefully evaluate financing options and ensure alignment with your values and long-term vision.

9. Maintain a Customer-Centric Focus: Growth shouldn't come at the expense of customer satisfaction. Prioritize excellent customer service, gather feedback, and adapt your offerings based on their needs.

Remember: Scaling is a journey, not a destination. Experiment, adapt, learn from setbacks, and celebrate your progress.

Real-Life Scaling Stories: Learning from the Masters

Let's glean insights from successful companies that navigated the scaling journey:

- **Warby Parker:** This online eyewear company started by selling directly to consumers through their website, scaling efficiently by leveraging technology and partnerships to expand their product line and reach.
- **Dropbox:** This cloud storage solution started with a simple referral program, incentivizing existing users to invite others, driving organic growth and reducing marketing costs.
- **Airbnb:** This hospitality platform empowered ordinary people to become hosts, creating a scalable supply chain of unique accommodations and disrupting the traditional hotel industry.

These are just a few examples. Analyze successful businesses within your industry, understand their growth strategies, and adapt them to fit your unique context and vision.

Beyond Scale: Building a Legacy that Matters

Scaling your business isn't just about numbers; it's about impact. Ask yourself: What legacy do you want to leave? How will your business make a positive difference in the world?

Remember, true success extends beyond profits. Integrate social responsibility and ethical practices into your scaling strategy. Give back to your community, advocate for positive change, and inspire others through your leadership.

A Final Note: Embrace the Climb, Together

Scaling your business is a thrilling yet challenging journey. Embrace the climb, celebrate small wins, and remember that you're not alone. Build a supportive network, learn from others, and leverage the power of collaboration to reach new heights. As Simon Sinek famously said, "Leadership is not about being in charge, it's about taking care of your people." Foster a culture of trust, empowerment, and shared purpose, and you'll not only scale your business but also build a legacy that inspires and empowers others.

>"The purpose of business is not just to make money; it is to make the world a better place." - John D. Rockefeller (with the caveat that ethical practices must underpin this approach).

CHAPTER 10:

Million Dollar Mindset: Developing Financial Habits for Success

Welcome, aspiring entrepreneurs, to the world of the Million Dollar Mindset ! While financial success isn't solely measured in monetary terms, mastering your financial well-being forms the bedrock upon which entrepreneurial dreams are built. This chapter equips you with the financial literacy, smart money management practices, and abundance mindset needed to fuel your journey towards success and financial freedom.

Beyond Basic Budgeting: Laying the Foundation

Let's dispel the myth that financial success is reserved for the privileged few. It's about developing awareness, making informed choices, and cultivating healthy financial habits. It's like building a strong house – you wouldn't start with the roof, would you?

1. **Embrace Financial Literacy:** Knowledge is power. Invest time in understanding financial concepts like income, expenses, investments, and debt. Seek resources like books, online courses, or workshops to expand your financial vocabulary and sharpen your decision-making skills.

2. **Track Your Money:** You can't manage what you don't measure. Start by tracking your income and expenses to

understand where your money goes. Utilize budgeting apps, spreadsheets, or simply a good old-fashioned notebook to gain clear insights into your financial habits.

3. Create a Spending Plan: Don't let your money control you; you control it. Develop a budget that aligns with your goals and values. Allocate funds for essential expenses, savings, and investments, leaving room for responsible enjoyment.

4. Embrace Delayed Gratification: While instant gratification feels good, long-term success demands patience and planning. Resist impulsive purchases, prioritize needs over wants, and invest in experiences that enrich your life rather than fleeting material possessions.

Remember: Building a strong financial foundation takes time and discipline. Celebrate small wins, stay committed to your goals, and remember, every step towards financial wellness brings you closer to your entrepreneurial dreams.

Building Your Money Machine: Smart Strategies for Growth

Now, let's explore some powerful strategies to propel your financial engine forward:

1. Automate Your Finances: Set up automatic bill payments and savings transfers to eliminate manual effort and ensure financial consistency.

2. Pay Yourself First: Treat your savings like a fixed expense. Allocate a portion of your income towards savings or investments before paying other bills, prioritizing your future self.

3. **Embrace Frugal Living:** Being frugal doesn't mean deprivation; it's about mindful spending. Explore cost-saving alternatives, negotiate bills, and find joy in experiences over material possessions.

4. **Invest for the Future:** Don't let your money sit idle. Explore various investment options based on your risk tolerance and timeframe, seeking professional guidance if needed. Remember, compound interest is your friend!

5. **Manage Debt Wisely:** If you have debt, prioritize paying it off with high-interest rates first. Develop a debt repayment plan and avoid accumulating unnecessary debt.

6. **Create Multiple Income Streams:** Diversify your income sources to mitigate risk and increase financial security. Explore freelancing, online businesses, or passive income options that align with your skills and interests.

Remember: There's no one-size-fits-all approach to financial success. Experiment, adapt strategies to your unique circumstances, and seek professional guidance when needed. The key is to be proactive, informed, and committed to your financial well-being.

Cultivating an Abundance Mindset: Beyond the Numbers

Financial success extends beyond numbers; it's about mindset and perspective . Here's how to cultivate an abundance mindset:

1. **Practice Gratitude:** Focus on what you have, not what you

lack. Express gratitude for your resources, opportunities, and the ability to create wealth.

2. Challenge Scarcity Beliefs: Reframe limiting beliefs about money into empowering affirmations. Replace "I can't afford it" with "I am worthy of abundance" and focus on possibilities instead of limitations.

3. Visualize Success: See yourself achieving your financial goals in your mind's eye. Create a vision board, write down your financial aspirations, and visualize yourself living the life you desire.

4. Surround Yourself with Positive Influences: Connect with individuals who share your financial goals and support your aspirations. Avoid negativity and surround yourself with those who inspire and motivate you.

5. Give Back: Generosity fosters abundance. Donate to causes you believe in, mentor others, and share your financial knowledge. Giving back fosters gratitude and attracts positive energy into your life.

Remember: An abundance mindset doesn't guarantee instant riches; it's about aligning your beliefs, actions, and energy with the creation of prosperity. Believe in your ability to achieve your financial goals, take consistent action, and trust that the universe conspires to support your dreams.

Real-Life Stories of Abundance: Inspiration from Success

Let's draw inspiration from individuals who cultivated an abundance mindset and achieved financial success:

Sara Blakely, founder of Spanx: From cutting off pantyhose feet to create her revolutionary product, Sara didn't let limited resources or societal norms hold her back. Her belief in her idea and unwavering determination fueled her journey to becoming a billionaire.

Oprah Winfrey: Overcoming poverty and discrimination, Oprah built a media empire through sheer hard work, resilience, and an unwavering belief in her potential. Her generosity and commitment to empowering others exemplify the true essence of abundance.

Chris Gardner, author of The Pursuit of Happyness: Homeless with a young son, Chris persevered through unimaginable challenges, fueled by his vision for a better life. His story reminds us that abundance can blossom even in the most trying circumstances.

These are just a few examples. Look around you, discover stories of individuals who defied odds and achieved financial success through a combination of smart strategies, a positive mindset, and unwavering belief.

A Final Note: Your Money Journey Begins Today

Remember, building financial success is a lifelong journey. Embrace the principles outlined in this chapter, be patient, learn from experience, and most importantly, never stop believing in your ability to achieve financial freedom and abundance. As Warren Buffett famously said, "The most important investment you can make is in yourself." Invest in your financial education, cultivate a healthy money mindset, and take action towards your goals every single day. With dedication and a commitment to growth, you'll unlock the power of the Million Dollar Mindset and pave the way for a future filled with prosperity and fulfillment.

>"Don't let money define you, but let it refine you." - Robert Kiyosaki

CHAPTER 11:

The Million Dollar Vision: Defining Your Success and Achieving It

Welcome to the final chapter of Mastering the Game. You've built a strong foundation, honed your skills, and cultivated the right mindset. Now, it's time to unleash the ultimate driving force - your Million Dollar Vision. This chapter empowers you to define your unique definition of success, set achievable goals, and craft a personalized roadmap to transform your vision into reality.

Beyond the Dollar Sign: Redefining Success

Forget the stereotypical image of mansions and yachts. True success is deeply personal, a vibrant tapestry woven from your values, aspirations, and dreams. It's about living a life that feels fulfilling, impactful, and aligned with your authentic self.

Consider Oprah Winfrey, whose definition of success transcends wealth. She prioritizes empowering others, creating meaningful connections, and leaving a lasting positive impact on the world. Or think of Yvon Chouinard, founder of Patagonia, who redefines success through environmental activism and building a sustainable business model.

Remember: Your "millions" might not be measured in currency; they could be moments of joy, meaningful connections, positive impact, or the freedom to pursue your passions. Define what success truly means to you, and let that vision guide your entrepreneurial journey.

Charting Your Course: From Dream to Roadmap

Now, let's translate your vision into a tangible roadmap:

1. Embark on a Vision Quest: Dedicate time for introspection. Ask yourself: What truly excites me? What impact do I want to create? What kind of life do I desire? Journal, meditate, visualize, and allow your authentic desires to emerge.

2. Craft Your Vision Statement: Articulate your ideal future in vivid detail. Describe your lifestyle, business impact, personal fulfillment, and the positive ripples your success creates. Make it specific, emotionally charged, and a constant source of inspiration.

3. Break Down Your Vision: Divide your long-term vision into smaller, achievable milestones. These become stepping stones on your entrepreneurial journey, providing a sense of progress and motivation.

4. Set SMART Goals: Each milestone requires SMART goals - Specific, Measurable, Achievable, Relevant, and Time-bound. Define clear objectives, track progress, and celebrate achievements along the way.

5. Choose Your Strategies: Research and identify the strategies, skills, and resources needed to achieve your goals. Attend workshops, read relevant books, connect with mentors, and invest in your continuous learning.

6. Embrace Flexibility: The entrepreneurial path is rarely linear. Be adaptable, learn from setbacks, and adjust your course as needed. Remember, your roadmap is a guide, not a rigid script.

7. Celebrate Every Win: Acknowledge and celebrate even small victories. Each milestone crossed fuels your momentum and reinforces your belief in your ability to achieve your dreams.

Remember: This roadmap is uniquely yours. Tailor it to your strengths, resources, and the ever-evolving landscape of your industry. Embrace the journey, trust the process, and enjoy the thrill of transforming your vision into reality.

Real-Life Visionaries: Inspiration for Your Journey

Let's draw inspiration from individuals who dared to dream big and turned their visions into reality:

Elon Musk: Driven by a vision of a multi-planetary future, he revolutionized industries with Tesla and SpaceX, defying naysayers and pushing the boundaries of what's possible.

Malala Yousafzai: Her unwavering vision for girls' education led her to become the youngest Nobel laureate, demonstrating the power of a passionate vision combined with relentless pursuit.

Muhammad Yunus: Driven by a vision of social and economic justice, he pioneered microfinance, empowering millions and proving that success can be measured in impact as much as profit.

These are just a few examples. Look around you, find individuals who dared to dream big and made a difference, and let their stories fuel your own journey.

Beyond Millions: Leaving a Legacy of Impact

Remember, true success extends beyond personal fulfillment. What legacy do you want to leave? How will your business contribute to a better world?

Consider Patagonia's commitment to environmental sustainability or TOMS'"One for One" model that donates shoes to children in need. Integrate social responsibility and ethical practices into your vision, leaving a positive impact that ripples far beyond your immediate success.

A Final Note: Dare to Dream, Dare to Achieve

Your Million Dollar Vision is your North Star, guiding you through challenges and illuminating the path towards a fulfilling and impactful life. Don't be afraid to dream big, set ambitious goals, and take action every single day.

As Henry David Thoreau said, "Go confidently in the direction of your dreams. Live the life you have imagined.

Embrace the journey, celebrate your wins, and remember, the greatest reward isn't the destination, but the transformation you undergo along the way. As Nelson Mandela eloquently stated, "It is not our abilities that limit us, but our doubts." Dare to believe in your vision, silence the inner critic, and unleash the unstoppable force within you.

Remember, you are capable of achieving more than you can imagine. The world needs your unique contribution, your spark of brilliance, and your unwavering determination to create a better future. So, embark on this exciting adventure, armed with your million-dollar vision, a strategic roadmap, and an abundance mindset. The world awaits your impact, and the only limit is the one you set for yourself.

>"The dream doesn't work unless the dreamer does." - John C. Maxwell

the ultimate reward isn't just reaching your personal "millions," but the profound impact you create along the way. As Nelson Mandela eloquently expressed, "It always seems impossible until it's done." So, go forth, dear entrepreneur, and turn your Million Dollar Vision into a reality that inspires, transforms, and leaves a lasting legacy for generations to come.

Visit "MINDS LIBRARY" on YouTube for all our value impacted Audiobooks for free.

Like, SUBSCRIBE to "MINDS LIBRARY" and do not forget to hit on that notification bell so that you will get access and won't miss out on our value impacted Audiobooks on our channel.

Over 1.5k Community members has joined

"MINDS LIBRARY" on YouTube. So to Join Visit us on YouTube and Click on SUBSCRIBE

https://youtube.com/@Mindslibrary

BOOKS BY THIS AUTHOR

Self Help Books (7 Books)

www.ingramcontent.com/pod-product-compliance
Lightning Source LLC
Chambersburg PA
CBHW070408230526
45471CB00006B/2711